Live Canon
2017 Anthology

First Published in 2017
By Live Canon Ltd
www.livecanon.co.uk

All rights reserved

© Live Canon 2017

978-1-909703-29-2

Live Canon

2017 Anthology

The poems in this anthology were longlisted for the
2017 Live Canon International Poetry Prize

Contents

The Dissolution of the Libraries   8
Emma Simon

Hardknott   9
Simon Stacey

Rivariations   12
Geraldine Clarkson

How to Recognise the Stars   15
Mark D. Cooper

International Trunk Call   16
Samuel Prince

Camera Obscura   17
Gillie Robic

earth and moon pull different ways Rebecca   19
Tim O'Leary

Zero-sum Game   21
Gregory Kearns

Blue   22
Amy Neilson Smith

Fancy Dress in the Time of Brexit   24
Astra Bloom

The Sewing Table   25
Marie Josephine Diamond

Ablaze at the World Museum, Liverpool   26
Pauline Rowe

Mussoorie - An Indian Cosmography   28
Will Johnson

Inventory. Books   30
Mark Fiddes

Smitten, Kitten   31
Alan Buckley

Here I Am, Father   32
Peter Jarvis

Homing brain   34
Claire Trevien

Aurora Borealis   35
Justin Hunt

Amsterdam, 1901   36
Kirsten Irving

Breakfast at Theresa's   38
Andrew George

The last to die   39
Alexander Velky

Postcards from my Father   40
Tessa Foley

The Great String   42
Lindsay Fursland

The Sounding Marsh   43
Oona Chantrell

Don't follow the white van man   44
Richard Carpenter

Offshore   46
Tim Dooley

Leaving-Do   48
Iain Batchelor

Do you remember those wild, out of control,   50
pre-referendum days? *Josephine Corcoran*

The English translation of an Indian horn on   52
the 25th May *Arji Manuelpillai*

Noah   55
Sophie Fenella

Butlins, Bognor 1964   58
Alison Falconer

Epitaph   60
Becky Edwards

Tax Return   61
Elaine Beckett

The Lost   63
Sarah Wimbush

Pansies   65
Gordon Fudge

As It Is   65
Kevin Scully

Working from Work   68
Andrew George

Passing the Ball   69
Konstandinos Mahoney

The Hold Days   70
Geraldine Clarkson

Jeanne d'Arc on Flight TK1828   71
Antony Mair

Women's Arts Alliance Exhibition   72
Caroline Gilfillan

Out of the Blue   73
Lesley Saunders

in the misperception of my life   74
Michèle Betty

Tied Up   76
Oliver Comins

In Crimson Boots   78
Jo Sanders

Homecoming   79
Mark Huband

Dancing The Harvest In   80
Brian Docherty

Empty Box (Death Of A Cat)   81
Arthur Fox

Hairy Panic   82
Matt Barnard

Among the Translators   83
David Underdown

On the journey home   84
Jack Houston

The Dissolution Of The Libraries
Emma Simon

Words whirled away   like thought untethering
itself.   Stand here — dugdeep in boneshells
of abandoned bookbanks — and hear
their *whisperlong*   as winds blow in.

The ransacked sky-stacks   row after row
reaching to a roofdome,   now rent weather-wide.
Mouldmaps inbloom   between bird shitsplat spines;
nestled nooks for house-spugs & mouserats.

Gone all the idolgold: the glimmerings
on paperthick and parch,   that flare, facelit,
matchbright —   magic as moonglare
suddenly uncloudclothed   —   picking out a path.

Wonder when whole worlds were ribbed in rhyme:
scriptsafe, bookbound.   A hoard of heartsong.
Secrets storied like spells   to ken, to keen,
to kindl   warmfire in winterdarks.

O weary word-wanderer   travelsore and tired
hopesmirched so homefar home.   Timesgone
when sounds ink-sketched slipt moutheasy
to meaning. Didn't fur tongue   taste foreignfull.

Hardknott
Simon Stacey

We are easily scared. Sure enough
It scared us: into an instant vow it won't again.

As steep as any road in England. And
Rain: pouring like a garden's bell-fountain

Down the tarmacked fells. All coming our way.
Watered, you could say, we left the inn. I drove.

The pass chucked altitude at us, my main worry
Rolling back. Only the car was sky blue,

While camber, one-direction rain, the leather-grip
And red-death signs screamed black percentages.

With your fear of heights (mine) – I want to call it
Falling-sickness – should anyone be surprised?

You don't do hills, but had the choice: the winding
Eighty miles of coast-road, or the watery one.

All afternoon, on Harter Fell, it threatened.
I panicked in the sliding mist, ducked Wainright's

Truer summit, but got down like Hansel
On his own, nudged either side by cairns

Oblivious of their stony treachery. I dried off
In the car. Love or fear put us in the lowest gear.

Height? What is this? If I looked out now,
Dead level, what angle would I have to

Bend to meet your four-foot eyes? The first up-slope
Your heart was somewhere, my eyes on the road.

I'm sure I prayed. At the hair-pin near the top
A Land Rover (or something big) surprised us.

Then the one-in-three, a water-slide, and brakes.
Gripped, I swear you clasped the wheels on the descent.

Strange, it works the other way with walking hills.
We are so different. It didn't stop you,

Either, spurning Duddon as escape-route.
On: another, just as high. And so on: down.

Wimps. But this I thought extraordinary:
Later a wife at work confesses candidly that her mad husband,

Around their marriage-time, would insist on getting her
To drive up Hardknott in a similarly tiny car.

Before she'd passed her test? She stalled.
The story was he made her keep her foot upon the brake

Whilst placing chocks behind cascading rear wheels,
Then jumped in, changing places. Off. Good grief.

There is a sad part: quite soon after she confided this,
He left her – with two children.

Went to teach in Abu Dhabi. Dry, flat. Just like that.
Apparently, their differences meant they could no longer

Share the driving. Thank God we're still together:

Taking different paths on foot, my fear of driving

Growing. And the brave? Just now on radio
I heard a widow tell, through tears, of her husband's love

For terrorists even, like his killer
In a hired London car: for everyone.

Tell me:
What is this fear I have? This love so high,
That many of us find as hard as mountains?

Rivariations
Geraldine Clarkson

I *The Ouse Is My (Unexpected) Home*

I slip into the day as into swish silk.
Up before anyone, digging out morning's moist
newness like potatoes. Green prickling
my nose, sharp as thorn. I head down the slope.
Hop. Down by the apple trees, down by
the apple trees. Skip.

The water is plated, a table set for tea.
One little white teacup for you, my dear.
A trembling, almost transparent, slice
of angel cake.

Icy green slink — *oh why did you* —
fugitive flurry, rattlesnake breath.
How roomy here, in this black heart.

II *Louis Limpopo Laments*

like an oiled clarinet, a bouncy bassoon,
with caulked cork on his back. A sulky slider
of green treacle, slow, with a sloe-gin kick,
all from one lung. Through desert and forest,
he's hippopotamussy. Has one ancient urgent
push to carry me home. Fever trees
make a low chariot. *Ain't going to
study war no mo'.*

III *Shelagh Shannon Shoulders the Cross.*

She batters rocks like crockery, brims.
From overhead (the familiar home-tug
gets you from all angles), you see she trails a mane
of porter-black, with its froth, and gullies of
ginger, jellied air. What did they all
want, my sorrows drowned. It's goodbye,
Muirsheen Durkin. *Going to lay down my*
burden, down by, down by. Pulling up
through bog and moor, potato land. Gliding by
strange new settlements, shiny acre gardens. Old
hurt. Work away now, work away. These rocks
seep secrets. Rough words into the night.
Someone who oughtn't to be there. Lies.
Something wrapped in a cloth entrusted
to the emerald stream.

IV *Mr Derwent*

How d'you do, my rushing gent, tawny-capped,
whiskers bristling, up at Howden, busy about
a northern agenda, along steep corridors,
ten thousand items to see to, circling the scree
and sparing a word to court the lady scar. Debrief
at Hathersage, healing rush down through
Matlock. Thick oak valleys. You try to hold it back
but you break out with such a brown surge.
Whip, slap. Mutate, flower into cotton and silk.
I follow in my head, on, on through rock
and lime and moor, always forward
with canny grit, brief circuits but blunt as a tongue.
The wind confounds you at Ambergate.
I spent two years trailing you
then wonder where you went.

V *Gave de Pau, Lourdes*

One leap down from the snows, and she pauses the tune
to pass the shrine — rheumy, watery place. Milk-green
with the sun on it, rising, full of lace.
October firebombing the trees.

So cold. The shock of contact – mother's blue
obliterates thought. Baby's legs working, treading air
in a jig of anticipation, little life held close, nut-heart
refixing itself to the tree, held hard, one flow.
Now nothing new will ever be the same again.

How to Recognise the Stars
Mark D. Cooper

We practised our indoor astronomy
with a nightlight when the weather was bad.
Once memorised, we took turns to rename
the constellations circling your bed,

letting the sleepless planetarium
brighten your wallpaper with doubtful tales.
Batteries lit an incandescent scrum
of love and grudges. We saw immortals

patrol the banks of star-swollen rivers
about to burst. Omens bloomed on the mirror.
Heroes sought refuge, tumbling in reverse
around a vase of stocks. But to admire

millennia passing with the slow collapse
of dust clouds into light was to make the silence
deafening, taste the curse on nervous lips
and polish our way of looking to a lens

that folded the room deeper inside
ourselves. For all its beauty, life will hurt.
There's nothing to do about it, though I've tried
drinking, prayer, aerobic exercise. The heart

opens to what it must. Our city rhymed
traffic and birdsong with impermanence.
Small passings came among great. We dreamt
in snapshots of a lifetime's spiralled dance.

Outside, the slowly disappearing stars
doubled the nebulae around your vase.
Then nothing was, not even our bodies
coupled beneath a swim of pinhole gods.

International Trunk Call
Samuel Prince

Pips in delayed intervals:
Operator damn you, patch me through.

Down to a week's antivirals —
febrile, early onset, nascent tick nicks.
Rabid runts chew on a kerosene rag.

Dig it: contractors, prospectors, the sound of drills,
embedded freelancers searching for a signal,
aqua-wealth mainlined somewhere else.
Pip   pip   pip.

What was it the whisky priest said?
Hope itself is the profoundest form of the sublime.
And what was it the leftist fixer said?
You're uninvited harvesters. What's yours was mine.
And what did the hophead psalmist see?
So many broken lines.

Pip   pip   breakthrough.
A three second delay, a daughter's voice.
The toil of cosmic hardware to keep connection —
less than a minute to make it count.

Baby, this is the realm of the river
and you know what that means:
botanical trips, banana beer as bad juju,
the native pastis as rocket fuel.
Never mention this fractured call.
Now, figure skate to school.

Camera Obscura
Gillie Robic

when I was small I never knew
I would grow this big
I'm in the way of the light

the old stories are twisted
into invisibility

I need the curve of wood under the arches of my feet
and the true names
that hold the parameters steady

if I lose concentration
the innocence of bird and brute will alter
the cheerful crackling on the hearth
and threaten

as the trees close in
small creatures crawl out of the floorboards
drop from the branches
stream away among the trunks
the roots the darkness

I am the darkest thing in here
whatever is visible
obscures everything else

the coloratura chimney screams
don't be fooled by the silence
the beast is out there

I can see the gleam
of its eyes reflected
in this small bottle
when I hold it away from the flames
if I see more I'm in trouble

tonight I sat down at the edge
of the clearing
pulled the long grass around me

when they burned it down
the trees facing me were charred and twisted
their far sides still green and lush

If I don't want to see
I should open my eyes

earth and moon pull different ways Rebecca
Tim O' Leary

fugitive penitent locked-out tied-in
you want the silence to snare me
like the guts of cage's 4' 33"
and there's nothing here but silence

nothing maturing no action untoward
nothing but what fills it
a sense of the past and a motion forward
to the couplings of another age

what determines the silence
on this wet afternoon
is the river's weight at spring high-tide
the heckling of rain on a rusty roof

and you losing yourself in dreams
of weather forming warmer fronts
as you feed the story that's undoing your life
to men who write down storms

and off you go again hoping
for unintended consequences
with that famous eye that doesn't bat a lid
in the camouflage and aliases
you invent to flesh out your denial
believing that the ice will melt
if the jetstream shifts

don't ambush the silence
it can't fight back
its preciousness is exactly in how it stands
open to violence
challenging spies undercover
in a system that beats up the tired and the quiet
we are spied upon to death
a death that's happy to wait
beyond the last interrogation of togetherness
beyond the last weak raised voice in the fertile valley
where silence is always ambushed.

Zero-sum Game
Gregory Kearns

"If the body is a light bulb and it burns out, does that mean there's no more electricity?" Joseph Campbell

Okay, I used to lie awake at night,
see faces push out from the dark.
I think I recognise those faces Milo
or at least the lights in those eyes.
If your eyes replaced mine Milo,
would anybody notice?

I'm still afraid of being asleep.
Your body heavy as a Mother's grief
I've been six months less than you have-not.
One life hides another life Milo
and in this case 'me' excludes 'you'.
Milo, at one point I knew your home.

I think I love you more than I love myself.
Milo, merciful soldier of the subjunctive tense.
I can't hear you but sometimes it's difficult
to know the difference between trying and learning.
It's the same difference between a match stick and a lit match
You're not the only ghost to cast shadows.

Blue
Amy Neilson Smith

Silk soft walls newly papered bright blue;
I can hear your Daddy and I laughing,
covered in slushy paste, smeared over
fingers and each other. Little balloons
dance on the borders, peopled with pirates.
If I listen hard enough I can hear you
laughing: maybe two, maybe three,
perfect, plump, kissable.

We didn't think you'd be a girl.

We didn't think you'd be born blue.

*

Beryl-ribbon boots, barely palm size;
I can still feel you; an adamantine softness,
covered in the uncontainable, smeared over
fingers and each other. Little people
toddle round shelves of toys; princes and pirates.
If I listen hard enough I can still hear you
laughing: maybe *Daddy,* just maybe *Daddy,*
perfect, plump, kissable.

We didn't think you'd be a girl.

We didn't think you'd be born blue.

*

Cerulean eyes; content with your soft teal;
I can almost touch skin, ascertain your heat;

covered in near-nakedness, smeared over
fingers and each other. Little portals
dilate: in pours, thighs; pupils and possibilities.
If I listen hard enough I can almost hear
you laughing: maybe look, just maybe see me,
perfect, plump, kissable.

We didn't think you'd be a girl.

We didn't think you'd be born blue.

Fancy Dress in the Time of Brexit
Astra Bloom

Let's go fabulous, let's go licksplit.
How else can we manage it?
I hatelove them all, so let's go play,
let's go Franglais, it gives guts.
Let's stun the creeps so old and done,
we'll wear masks, we'll rise above.
You be le Owl from the charmant English nursery rhyme,
I'll be une petite bat, not a pussy cat, all in black for my
grief, and because I feel French. And you with your round
eyes, that taste for a mouse under a table, that swoop you have;
you go to town, while I in this nuit tie knots above their heads, fly
black spells, remember them all manner of bad things pre the 1970s
(Quel horreur!) in my favourite antique blouse with the wide sleeve wings;
finding by sound, blinded by les yeux of this do, hiding from Beth and all her
not-bein-funny-but stories, and Brace (who's called that?) with his picklish dickish
afternoon breath, and his big stiff politics, which is all how he gets sex, and does nothing,
and is lonely. Mon amour, let's go, but fly soon. Christ, and we must seal our lips with
hope and wine kisses — Je ne veux pas any bloody Great Britain discussions. *Arses*!
Je déteste ceux que j'aime! Who throws a fucking fancy dress party at a time like this?

The Sewing Table
Marie Josephine Diamond

A soft pinewood table
scored with needle scars
was salvaged from an eastside sweat shop
a locked airless space where sewing girls
in flight from pogroms in Poland, Russia and Moldova
dreamed of America's table of plenty.

Recycled for dining in a Tribeca loft
it could seat twelve but fell short
and stood unused along a white brick wall
as worms invisibly threaded themselves
into its wooden legs shredded by cats
clawing for prey at unremembered trees

In the interests of hygiene, minimalism
principles of Feng Shui and traveling light
it was chopped up for firewood
ashes for the second millennium
of mass migrations, bombed out homes
and abandoned tables blasted into trash.

Ablaze at the World Museum, Liverpool
Pauline Rowe

after Gerald Stern

Trying to comprehend, say how, say who, say why – say all of us
hiding in healing masks, dancing – say space travel, say
genetics

learning all the symbols on the Rosetta Stone, say writing
hieroglyphics
reciting the book of the dead.

                         We become Vietnamese water
puppets
our movements curious, carved, our colours burning
with the secrets of Buddha's mouth

                          we adored him
walking through the universe painting with our dreams
calling out like ancient birds

all this time and we don't know
why we're here.

We think hard in fish scales, in snakes, arrowheads,
bones in rocks, sundials.

We carry them home invisible on the bus,
scatter them on the number 18

to Bootle and Tuebrook
take them with our pills and daily injections of sleep

carrying the earth's spectrum

sculpting dark fires

until the embers heat our hands

leap and crack, spark upwards
as the colours
                leaving our souls alight,

pour from us
                outwards
                        flaming
                                ablaze.

Mussoorie – an Indian Cosmography
Will Johnson

Today Indra has decided on rain
but who can track his real intention?
Wet settles on the rhododendron's sheen
with a leopard sound, one spotted paw
before the next.
Will the cloud never lift? Shall I never
see the mountain goddess
draw her famous bow?

Have patience . . . In time all these sewers,
shanties, glamour queens and gods shall be reabsorbed
into the forty-four winks of a submariner slug –
or a deep-sea deity, if that's how you read it –
your body too in the silt of that flawless mind.
Keep patience . . . For after a millennium,
multiplied by a cipher beyond computation,
all shall be reborn and remade,
not least the mountain goddess and her bow.

But in the interim – which may
or may not turn out to be ours –
we should go to the square at cow dust hour,
while the road is still passable,
and catch the crystal coach to Dehra Dun.
Either that or prepare to be cocooned
by a three-day storm,
spinning like a discus on a god's finger
round Nanda Devi – 'prepare'
in the sense of 'do nothing'
apart from agree to be typecast,
feet up first on the sahib-white veranda.

So what's it to be? Let me know before you step
into the lane where, last time I listened, an animal
was growling like an unfed belly across the sub dark
of the entire continent – let me know now, because
it may be that by going down we shall encounter nothing but air,
where souls speak with tongues, while the body stays leery,
and we need to prepare all possible ends,
all limits to being, all bad incarnation.

The alternative, and an analogue of home,
is to lie in a Raj-filled graveyard,
above a Raj-built house,
pre-empting our turn,
while down there, in the heat,
they suppose it their birth right –
the unexplained body, the inexplicable soul.

But then again, it may be time well wasted –
time in which we can attempt, in a final throw,
to make ourselves clearer
and not make clearer seem less true –
hanging on
until all that we've lost
gets lost itself, and that god we've ignored
since the whole thing began
comes sauntering through,
one spotted paw before the next.

Mussoorie – a Himalayan hill station, popular with the British Raj
Indra – the ancient Indian god of the weather
Nanda Devi – a Himalayan peak; also a goddess
Dehra Dun (pr. Doon) – the town and rail terminus in the plain below
Mussoorie

Inventory. Books
Mark Fiddes

When the removal men come, they use cotton gloves and masks for
the books.
"It's the dust," he shakes his head, like we were in Nagasaki instead
of Tooting.
Penguin classics, their black spines cracked with effort, slip in beside
Elmore Leonard.
It's Boll to Cocteau in the next carton and a dog-eared frottage of
existentialists.
Elsewhere, Middle Earth meets middle class. Narnian queens spoon
Truman Capote.
Carver should have his own box but he's joined by Tour Guides from
The Lonely Planet.
Aristotle, Hobbes and Locke nuzzle Jean Rhys smelling of church and
whisky bottles.
Thin, interesting pamphlets from the Poetry Book Fair jam between
Chekhov's women
and fifteen Oxford Histories that remain impregnable as Dame Vera's
bluebird cliffs.
All the damned verse cramps up in sizes so diverse they say it must be
flat-packed.
Then they're gone - in their tottering truck with the boxes stacked in
sugar cubes.
Off to storage with the rest of us for an uncatalogued period of sorting
shit out
while our dust still grips the empty shelves like finger marks left on
a window ledge.

Smitten, Kitten
Alan Buckley

In my book *smite* is pure Biblical, the way
it channels no fluffy deity but fearsome
Jehovah – all wrath and thunderflash, black
clouds rolling aside to reveal the big G –

so I'm puzzled why *smitten* should indicate
something as light as that first flush, that hint
of blushing when the other's thought of, that
Has she Liked my last status update, crafted

partly (well wholly) with her in mind, has she
replied to my faux-casual lunch invite,
though part of the deal when it comes to the heart
is the way all sense of proportion gets lost,

like Harry Beck's audacious diagram,
or Alice's underground *Drink Me* trip,
so while your youth / petite frame might summon
the word, you can't be belittled with *kitten,*

you're more a snow leopard, and if – meeting
in a deli near Jericho, chewing the fat
over tofu curry – your hand, gesturing
to make a point, should brush my forearm, I'd feel

the force of a swipe from that animal's paw,
no doubt, it's the law of nature, of big cats /
desire / God, they may not mean us any harm
but we're struck, struck dumb all the same.

Here I Am, Father
Peter Jarvis

I know the neighbours' tree has a hand in things,
a branch rubbing against the open window
of my upper verandah room, clacking its pods
all night. Does this trigger the dream?
Mole-rats, furless, pink and phosphorescent
squirm in phalanxes over my bedroom floor,
toothy snouts quivering at the scent of prey –
then father's voice from the foot of the stairs
(he is after me) sternly commanding –
sea-hares are glued together in a pearly mat of spawn
tethered to the lagoon's rushy fringe.
Will the mole-rats syphon up the sea-hares?
How do I dream always of clashing things?
I know what I did today to anger father:
rode too far out of town to go fishing.
Below the spillway I caught a hatful of tiddlers,
then a barbel. I brought them home stiff and stinking.
Sea hares are hermaphroditic. Mole-rats
starving in their runs eat their own faeces.
I must check beneath my bed for scorpions
then spring with one bound through the French doors
into the study. It is like a dim hole in space.
I look down. My legs end in a giant foot
stuck in sea-hare spawn. I rotate on the spot –
a slow spinning-top. I cannot go back to bed.
I cannot get to the head of the stairs. Father calls.
O father, I can go no farther. The rosy curtains
are open. The cloud moon disrobes itself,
lets light glint off the bookcases, exposes
the big desk's blotter, the typewriter,
the humidor, the cylindrical ebony ruler,
manilla folders piled, pink-ribboned,

full of terrible secrets spied into by me –
that body on the slab, knife in its skull,
that croc-ravaged corpse hauled from a river-bank.
Mother said never to open his briefcase.
But I did. And with my sister picked
through scores of inquest photographs.
I pull free of the resinous gloop – the force
tumbles me to the head of the staircase.
"Time is of the essence" is his lawyer-speak.
Arms outspread I dive from the top to crash
at his feet. I've made it! "Here I am, father.
I've wound myself into a ball for you."
The toe-caps of his shoes are faintly dusty.

Homing brain
Claire Trevien

It was that time of night when my brain speaks French
but my tongue spews wine, and the weather speaks emoji,
but the streets speak Latin, and my phone is speckled
with the language of my body leaning on it unlocked.

And I swayed towards home, half-hero half-blurred,
stomping with each step on another of the pavement's seams.
One grey operation after another bubbled beneath me,
puddles of asphalt stabbed with wild weeds.
And then here – the surface flaked past pain,
allowed a shoal to bare its back, unrolled
its fish scales beneath my feet – and I knew more
than anything that just a few more steps would do it.

Aurora Borealis
Justin Hunt

Phones rang that evening, house to house:
the Northern Lights! A rare sight
on the southern plains. We piled

into cars and pickups, caravanned north
to the treeless edge of town — my parents,
sister and I, all those prairie dwellers

I'll never forget. We parked and got out,
right-side wheels to the ditch. We knotted
in silence, craned into the cold expanse

of a sky we couldn't fathom and gave
no thought, none at all, to the grace
from which priests and preachers claimed

we'd fallen: some lost, virginal place,
some spotless sanctum high above.
No, that night we peered into pink swirls

and turquoise shudders, the amethyst
cavern of a moonless winter night.
We shivered in wind, in the gust of our sin —

the dust of a dirt road soiling our shoes.

Amsterdam, 1901
Kirsten Irving

> *Van Helsing broke the silence by asking Arthur, 'Answer*
> *me, oh my friend! Am I to proceed in my work?'*
>
> *'Do as you will, friend. Do as you will. There can be no*
> *horror like this ever any more.'*
>
> Dracula, *Bram Stoker*

Professor, do you ever think of the past
as a grey dog, that curls in a snooze at your feet,
but may any moment spring out of suspension,
its paws on your chest and its jaws wide open?

Perhaps for you, friend, it is more a fine mist
that hangs like lace or corner cobwebs
in every room, that does no harm really, just
shimmers and shies in the breeze or the storm.

Or a bat, its hands quite as long as its body,
with a thousand nights sewn in its memory pouch.
That gobbles down lives like mouthfuls of flies
and is wrapped up in leaves by the dawnbird reel.

Good Sir, I feared death once; a frog in the garden
half-halved by our kitten. I brought down the spade
then I whined like a wolf till my mother came running.
The cat sat in innocence, eyes like the moon.

Do not tell my uncle, the pastor, but some things
should stop with the final fat sob of the heart.
Man is one of them. That which we'd kill to have back
we must kill when it answers our heartbroken knock.

We make sense of the end any way that we can,
as petering trails in the tabletop dust.
As loss, perhaps love. Here English fails me.
Perhaps, Sir, you know of the right word in Dutch.

Breakfast at Theresa's
Andrew George

Do I want a soft-boiled Brexit?
She dipped a soldier in her yolk.
I'd love an over-easy Brexit.
She chuckled softly at her joke.

A coddled Brexit for the people?
A Brexit Royale for the Queen?
She fiddled with an errant pearl.
Perhaps a Brexit Florentine?

Basted, scrambled, lightly poached?
She flexed a kitten-heel at me.
A home-grown Brexit Arnold Bennett?
A fishy Brexit kedgeree?

She fixed me with a piercing stare
And hacked a hunk of barley-bread.
What do you want? she didn't ask.
I feel like toast I might have said.

The last to die
Alexander Velky

for FM-2030

Today the last to be allowed to die
Will say her words and give the nurse the nod.

She thinks she's going to a better place;
Though we suspect, she hasn't used the word.

What death is we now never hope to prove;
But pestilence and famine were just foils

To its brief mastery of humankind.
Now we are faced with many meaner trials:

What living is, we've none of us found out;
But now we've outlawed death we'll have the chance

To design a destiny befitting
Of our race. And many centuries hence

We'll still speak of how, once upon a time,
The last to be allowed to die were wrong

To upset our young unanimity,
To try to keep our siblinghood hamstrung.

Remember, our ancestors once looked up
Presuming they could pluck stars from the sky.

For far too long we've failed to question "How?"
And wasted far too many breaths with "Why?"

Postcards from my Father
Tessa Foley

My Daddy, he left me there under a tree,
To grow up in the dapple with the fruit to break teeth in,
Alone in the crib.
I rattled like mad so he'd hear a pure bell, buy and sell,
Off he swept, up the branches and into the sky.

But I must confess, he sends postcards and I, I have
A teddy from each fifth of the world and I shoot
An inch taller,
Waiting for mail. By myself, I have found a yellowish trail,
Squirming away from each passing touch.

I am so much discovered by grown-ups, I find.
With my spine in a brace, facing forward forever, not
Hearing a sound,
They give me notice, like Daddy who left without tears
But rolling keep left signs aflame in his eyes.

Whilst he trips to the moon, I'm marooned in the red,
My plot is too buried, down under the gum tree,
With disease in the roots,
I jack up my boots and go hiking in mud where my name
Has been questioned and stamped in and spread.

Feeling dead, hearing birds chant in branches above my cold crown,
I am down, paid in pink sweeties to hush on my lips,
And staring at drips,
On back windscreens to count out the secs, stone-handed, felled wrists
'Round their shoulders, I'm the shallowest notch on the post.

I just watch as my postcards thumb by, each tiny hitchhike,
A view with a click that's not the latch on my door.

They adore me,
They say and I can only believe, don't make like the gum tree,
Don't leave. They don't leave.

The Great String
Lindsay Fursland

So what happened was this. Simon said
all we needed was string and two cans,
for a telephone: baked beans
or golden syrup – there was no audible difference.
We had lots of string which was lucky
because Simon said his parents were taking him
to Australia – the North Eastern bit,
otherwise it wouldn't have stretched.

Simon would describe everything, his voice fuzzy
like a tiny dalek; coming and going
on waves of faraway, Simon says
the Coral Sea is butterfly-blue
with an underwater hedge that blushes and breathes.
Even in the moonshine, Simon says,
you can hear it sigh.

And *The Great String* is venerated for a while,
though people who happen to live on one side
begin to other the others. Then, it gets cut
by some border guards, who machete anything
which smacks of contact; I have to schlep
halfway across Mozambique to fix it.

And then, people become fanatically
anti-string; the world is growing up
and growing out of wonders…
As Simon and me are getting on too,
we feel obliged to hang up our telephone.
Funny: nowadays texters and facebookers
are shrinking the planet to a confessional.
Yet we were the pioneers! Simon and me.

The Sounding Marsh
Oona Chantrell

Cock an ear to the flurry of wings, a susurration
in the grass, the wind's low vowel funneling down the
esplanade. Shingle's wistful soul-song. Who can name
this raft of small white flowers swaying to the pulse of the under-
tow: they mass here incognito, starry bog-blooms
moored on slender lines. The warbler's young chitter
in the stemmy nests but keep mum when you draw close.
Plumed, neck-bent reeds seethe like broody swans.
                                        Fathoms rush
the tidal fringe. This is the high: breathless, blind and fore-
ordained to roll over the marginal life of the marsh,
scour and sift the palisade, the chalky claque
of oyster-shells submerging tiny cries. The sandbank
undermined, must slide away
and the record of the shore be wiped clear. Listen well
to the waves' encyclical: all sound is air.

Don't follow the white van man
Richard Carpenter

our bats have it right and find their way without collision.
We're one of several old farmsteads
with 'High Roans this or that' as a house name,
all at the southern boundary of the parish
where the Howardian Hills peter out into the Vale of York
and The Minster is our lodestone.

Don't be dependent on the vagaries of deliveries
knocking on our neighbours' doors.
Don't trust a SatNav —
it's a case of rubbish in means rubbish out.
Google maps won't help,
nor Parliament's Petition Map
which shows true-blue Ryedale is up there with the rest
to demand a say on who our Queen may entertain.

So how can I help you come to tea?
You might speak with ghosts of felons
who swung from boundary gallows,
or follow the King's Court hunting in his forest,
hitch a lift on a narrow boat up the Foss to the clay pits,
then trudge a mile south on Shanks's pony,
but the lock gates are broken, the river's silted.

Most posties and taxi drivers know the way,
everyone knows Pigotts scrapyard down the road
or the Tannery site leathered with 52 new houses.
One mile past The Ship,
then humpy bridge and cattery
with a turning down Pottery Lane for blackberries,

the car graveyard, York City sign.
Pass that, bear right with the road,
check your speed
and the rear-view mirror for boy-racers up your bumper —
roadkill graces all our verges,

turn first right into the yard,
mind the cat jumping shoulder high to catch a peacock.

Or in April grow some wings and fly,
follow the swallows coming home for summer —
they were here long before us and have a faultless map.

Offshore
Tim Dooley

'Ahoy', the sailor calls, '*Ahoj!*'
paddling his kayak downriver
a million metres from the sea.
Are those gulls or swifts following him
shadowed by the repurposed tower?

In the stone town, arches of stone
fan out above with peach shades
of sunlight streaming through the glass.
It is a long afternoon but not endless.

Look here is a picture of Barbara
Radziwill – pale, bejewelled and
not long to live. And, look, the ash
of Monet's cigarette refuses
to fall as he outstares his canvas.

The girls and boys of the village
rocked in their two-seater swings.
The city's steam-whistle reached them
slowly through the woods and lanes.

Our bridges cross rivers whose courses
have shifted. Warehouses turn into galleries.
It's pleasing to loosen the ties
of where we came from, replacing *syke*
and *sheugh* with *biro brio samizdat*.

Memorial plaques glitter in the
gap-toothed streets of renamed districts.
We follow the shifting electric display
spread out in the blood-streaked sky.

Hoardings appear with dates picked out
in a lightbulb array. 1848 and
Lajos Kossuth feels the century
turning against him. 1898 and
General Blanco announces *El Desastre*.

And Jean-Jacques is still botanizing near
Ménilmontant, caught in a reverie
between that which is no longer
and that which is often not to be.

How can one not look back on the
closed train, the manifesto lacking
a clause, an advancing *popolo*
chanting to an old Lombard tune?
Glories lost to a poundshop Gloriana.

Where are the accordions and clarinets
or has something already happened
so we hardly recognise these buildings:
town hall, hospital and school?

Why only trombones and a bass
drum, as we view from the stern
of the ferry the coastline slipping away?

Leaving-Do
Iain Batchelor

Not till I, blind-bellied and battle-robed
Have pointed out and consequently quaffed the froth —
Mingling, briny buzz-strobed
And cheshire-grinning, winning formula of She —
My petal, my tether, my town, not till then

shall I bid goodbye.

The tip-top tiles of the town I rip down, barking biting
The copper black road away. Drinking down the wives' tales
drier —
Keen as a fly on the turn, I'm searching — for that home-hearth fire.

That singular vein, a murmur in the whisper of that rumour,
Going around in the street below, believed to be the heart of her.

The tick-tock toll to tell me she'll miss me
When I'm gone to the city down South,
Grinding me like a mouth and inside out — seems wherever you go
It just changes how you're chewed, being spewed
From this home to that. This house to that. It's good that you're sat.

On the chair, on your plinth, in the Marina
Peering into the fibres of the air — All I get is your stare —
Asking you for guidance I would sooner summon clouds
To come down and wash all my ties away.

Your magnificence now a shroud, concealing present passing
daytimes.

We, the current crew of your life house eternal,
Privately yearning for bookended plaques upon the salt-blown wall.

We are coasting through a myriad of woods on the water —
Knots gripping taughter, the reflections nipping at our heels.

The pangs of memory forgotten: bound, constricted by eels.

I love you. My petal, my tether, my ton, I am longing
To see you bloom, to view the arc of your plume.

For I shall never age anymore, I'll sit in the shallow surges
Where I should have stayed, the night I went wandering for
your Pulse. The night I consulted the
man in the Marina.

Do you remember those wild, out of control, pre-referendum days?
Josephine Corcoran

When learner drivers raced down the hard-shoulder
And horses rampaged in the bus lanes?
And toddlers ran amok in shopping centres –
They were unreined!!
And air traffic control was at breaking point
So the skies teemed with airplanes
And hot air balloons set fire to the tree tops
And crashed into picnics
And you couldn't see two feet in front of you
For the peasoup of sausage rolls and tartan rugs
And it wasn't even regulation tartan!!

Do you remember our hair was so fly away
It could've reached outer space?
And there were no hidden control panels in underwear
And throngs of bra-less women ran on beaches – it was chaos!
And weeds sprouted from pavements
And children swirled in playgrounds like unlicensed
fireworks

And nobody kept to the menu or the timetable or the order of service
And everyone swam freestyle
And you couldn't move in the sea for fishing boats and lilos
and pedalos
And we needed to take back control.

And immigrants raced down the hard shoulder
With two council houses each on their backs
And crashed into benefit offices
And never spoke about sausage rolls

(Which made us feel so uncomfortable)
And they set fire to all of the waiting lists
And ran amok through hospitals and schools and workplaces
Stealing our jobs and our beds and our coat pegs
And you couldn't see two feet in front of you
For the peasoup of immigrants.

The queues at the supermarket were at breaking point.
The skies were teeming with immigrants.
You couldn't move in the sea for immigrants
And immigrants swam freestyle on the beaches
And immigrants sprouted through cracks in the pavement
And you couldn't walk without stepping on immigrants

And nobody kept to the facts or statistics
And everyone kept to the slogans
And the truth was so fly away
And headlines rampaged.

The English translation of an Indian horn on the 25th of May
Arji Manuelpillai

Good morning world

Goodbye wife

I'm leaving

See you soon

I'm beside you

Behind you

I need another inch of room

I'm coming round this bend

Are you coming round the bend?

Hurry up

Don't rush me

I think that is my friend

Excuse me to a cow

Get a move on to a human

Push over to a goat

Budge up to a camel

Watch my bloody car

You're reversing far too close

Watch my wing mirror

That's my bumper

Now it's broke

I'm overtaking

Undertaking

On the pavement

Celebrating

Are you waiting

Please jump in

Please jump in

Pretty lady looking good

I'm driving here

You're driving near

There's a problem with your bloody ears

Police up there!

Change your gear

I'd go faster if I could

Turn your lights on

Turn your lights down

I'm whizzing through this red

Move over truck

I'm driving here

Use that lane instead

You'll clip my wheel

You've clipped my wheel

Shit, I've lost control

Tell my wife I love her

I'm falling off this road

I've fallen off the road i've fallen off the road i've fallen off the

Noah
Sophie Fenella

Bring peace to us and to all
I mouth at the cat, who accepts
her fate and walks with quiet cool
across a burning border.

I look for the giraffe and see
he is at my window, *Giraffe,* I say,
go easy, be sure to kiss the family
in the house on the corner.

The corner, that is not a corner,
was once a meeting point
for children, now a hole
hides hair and Lego, in the belly
of this apocalypse.

The horse is here, brilliant, brave,
be strong, I say but she needs no
instruction, her back understands
the weight of falling bricks

and I cannot reassure her but try,
nevertheless, to promise
there will be no division, this time.

She nods, showing awareness
of the city streets — sick
with grease. And to her maternity
I add a woollen blanket. *I hear*
the frost is really kicking in,
she gets it, and goes on her way.

I call the robins, I call them
by their name. They land
at my feet, ready, sweet.
You know what to do,

I say, playing the cool guy
and off they fly fixing potholes
with kisses. Oh Man,
the modest stroke
of their wings,
the flight path, the skyline.

Next comes the eagle
dressed in feathers
the colour of sparrows skin,
feign tears as morning song,
I instruct without knowing
the eagle is a professor
of healing.

I ask the shark if he would mind
participating in
what I hope is
the start of a new world.

The shark is a great rock
of calm in my bedroom. This
is the most important moment
of my life;

the shark knows it and beckons
to the window. I lay him down
armed with a rifle.

I'm alone now. I talk loneliness

with the wall, run naked
out the door; as if I could mute
a community hall
of inflammatory slogans.

Exhausted — I wait and expect
a mention in tomorrow's news.

Or do I stand watching an army
of tanks descend on farmhouses
before pressing my palm
to my forehead as each animal
arrives — battered, crying
their own forgotten name.

Butlins, Bognor 1964
(Or, How my sister survived childhood)
Alison Falconer

Computers are the size of rooms
There's no TV 'til afternoon
But in Butlins pool in my rubber ring,
Plastic parrots match the echoing
Jungle screech of voices, I am six and
There is no better thing.

In the basement bar attached
Carol flicks her filter tip,
Her hopes of romance curling slowly into ash.
Behind the glass the bottom halves
Of ghostly children glide
Blue hued by aquarium light.

Twenty three and still at home
While other girls have rings and loans and prams
They look so cute in pictures or asleep.
One, underwater, makes a face.
She hopes a moment's all it takes
To turn things round; a moment's grace.

Meanwhile, pinned down by thrashing feet
Limbs cold and panic rising as you can't
Baby fingers blunting on the tank
Your face pressed like a catfish cleaning glass

You're praying harder than you do each night
for God to cure the deaf and blind
Which he hasn't yet but a miracle's required and
Now would be the time.

And on the other side, the adults
You've been taught will keep you safe
Are busy with their drinks, their books
Each other, as they, start to fade.

By the door, Jim holds his stomach in,
Chats to the Red Coat in confiding tone
And wishes he was younger now
The war's long gone and all the world but he is moving on
Remembers he said he'd watch the kids,
Glances at the tank, job done, he thinks.

And if time, at that moment stopped, the world would shift
Would tear... an irreparable rift between here and there,
But one small boy learns how to swim.

You push up as the pressure lifts
Gasp chlorined air, in this crowded space
Your life an unexpected gift
Random as a moment's grace.

Carol orders a Nescafe,
Unaware of the latte, cappuccino, unemployment still to come
A different barman clears her glass away
A ring to match complacent face: "Are you alright?" he says

Jim, suddenly aware of being old,
Heads off looking for his wife,
While I paddle oblivious in my rubber ring
Dreaming of an adventurer's life.

And you? Still shaking, cold, distressed,
You do the only thing kids can do,
Wait to see what happens to you next.

Epitaph
Becky Edwards

A walk through a backwater graveyard.
"This one's a sad one", you say,
And point to the corner where, unkempt,
Inscriptions have faded away.
"But no", I reply, "I'd prefer that":
The fizzing and hiss of my hours,
The splutter of dates and thin letters
Rubbed out by the wind. And for flowers,
Whoever is buried beneath them
Has this to lament their whole loss:
A firework explosion of lichen,
The faint decoration of moss.

Tax Return
Elaine Beckett

You are not a fool.
    You have fitted cupboards.
Yes, you've attempted to use a password without
    a user ID
several times, like an animal exploring
    the use of a primitive tool –
typing it in, leaving the other box empty,
    tapping, typing, leaving,
tapping. Persisting –
    just like Sally and Jonathan must have done
for the person who took their photographs
    for this leaflet, entitled;
'Slim and Trim in 28 Days'
    which you should not be reading
at the moment. Yes, it explains how to do
    a 'Squat Jump'.

    They probably felt a sense of unease
that after all their success
    it had come to this. Yes,
it is your fault: everyone knows to keep user IDs
    and passwords together in
sensible places, like Sally and Jonathan
    probably do.

Although Sally and Jonathan more likely
        have someone to do all of this
for them. They wouldn't be seen dead at three
        in the morning fretting
over a tax return, wondering why they
        are poor when they had
all the advantages the 20th century could possibly
        offer and now they can't even
complain because so many young people
        are heading towards far worse
situations, like competing with robots.
        Yes, imagine that:
imagine having to compete with a machine
        when all you want to do is
                fall in love.

The Lost
Sarah Wimbush

At the unveiling of the restored Lovers statue
outside The Staff of Life pub, 'All You Need Is Love'
playing by the Beatles, Margaret lingered once again —
the golden couple married at the pelvis, giant limbs
restructured, fibreglass skin resprayed...
                              there was a time
Margaret wore rollers beneath her headscarf
at the pickled onion factory behind Ford of Britain,
her nan and mam over the other side of the Don
at Crompton Parkinsons, swapping radio batteries
for .303 rifle ammunition then fluorescent tubes.
After her Friday shift, Brenda splashed out on
cheap as chips cod at Doncaster market served by Lesley
daubed in sky blue eyeshadow *ya right ma love?*
Elsie's grand-kiddies scrubbed up nice
while she minded them on Saturdays at Greyfrairs Baths,
changing them in poolside cubicles,
all their worldly goods in one wire basket, her youngest
Wendy on overtime at Brindon Ropes,
their cables still lowering men down shafts –
that manriding accident at Bentley pit
the seven lads who never came back – while at Pegler
Kevin Keegan began to make a name for himself.
And across Doncaster Carr the Travellers and Gypsies
pitched up with the wily hares and kingfisher flits
while the filthy rich lorded-it-over in NCB's Coal House
and Plant apprentices escaped at snap time in packs;
young and fit and sweet with sweat and engine oil,
green overall sleeves tied around their waists
eyeing the typists on lunch breaks who breathed
into pencil skirts at Chelsea Girl, then a quick shop
at Hillards before they all clocked back on.

Town always chocka: buses stuck in traffic
Rovers playing Barnsley FC, or Leger week fair;
spinning waltzers and gobsmacked goldfish
or that airshow malarkey at Finningley.
Gooin' round Donny town Satdy? Lager,
lager and lime, lager and black, lager bitter,
Lambert and Butler, The White Bear,
The Old Volunteer, The Yorkist, King's Head,
Nag's Head, Main Line, Romeo and Juliet's,
real ale at the Hallcross, bikers in Beethams,
The Bistro for a friend of a friend's wedding,
brandy and Babycham on special occasions,
a curry at the Indus; *good evening ladies.*
And inside the Arndale an eighteen year old girl
waiting for her boyfriend beneath the Lovers –
like birds in a cage
water streaming down gilded wires
fingertips reaching for the sky.
How their fibreglass feet were shattered
by the lump hammer, how they were rocked
and ripped away by developers then salvaged
for a backhander and planted
like an autumn maple, in a garden, in Bessacarr
and forgotten,
                          till now, outside Waterdale:
limbs splayed, bodies still joined at the hip in an X
heads flung back, the sky grinding across them
and the model villages
and the churches selling carpets
and the factories turned call centres,
the school yards, the ginnels, the smokeless chimneys
and beneath them, beneath all that, those lost men
and all that blackness still down there.

Pansies
Gordon Fudge

I bought her some flowers by chance
I didn't realise until I was done

I gave them to her half playfully
She didn't realise what I'd done

She put them to one side distracted
She didn't realise what she'd done

I took them home to save them
She didn't realise they were gone

I potted them on the front step
I was pleased with what I'd done

Every day my true love went past them
I was not sure she knew what I'd done

In the spring her bulbs grew through them
And then I knew that we were done

As It Is
Kevin Scully

There are wide worldly wonders in the shed —
The rake, the mower, the catcher for the grass.
All sit in readiness for Saturdays of work —
The initial pooch-poo patrol, the petrol from the can
To top up the tank, tiny as it is,
Before making off to mow it neat.

'Because untidiness, son, is far from neat
And discipline ensures disorder is shed
In a whirlpool of wild energy that is
Like our days, as the Psalmist says, but grass.
For we do how little or how much we can
In love, in leisure, in play, in work.'

And I suppose I can call it work —
This turning of long turf into neat
Lawn. Clippings, edgings, trimmings can
Be cast on the compost pile by the shed,
A Shard-like monument of grass
That eventually packs down to one and is

At one by and in itself. That's what it is.
Sweat certainly. Toil and tears. No blood. But work
All the same. In total worth a neat
Five dollars in coins and notes, grass-
Green twos and brownish ones. All shed
In playful pocket money. Do with it what you can

Before the next pile-up of dog shit can
Sour the happiness of seeing the yard is
Clean and clipped. All the tools are back in the shed
Where they can rest and rust till put back to work

In the cycle that renders this small universe neat
And tidy. Until man and machine are put out to grass.

Imagine concrete capping all this. No grass
To cut, no flipping clippings to rake, no can
To fill with fuel. Just all sweet and neat,
Done and dusted. A delightful task this is
Without coughing or hacking or the spit. No work
Inside or outside this bloody shed.

Cast all cares away. Let them be shed.
Lay down your life, your love, your work.
Let nature alone to be itself. As it is.

Working from Work
Andrew George

I unset the alarm and let myself in.
Every two weeks I change the code.
I read the junk mail, choose where
to make tea. I dust the kettle.
No-one steals the milk.
Even dark chocolate Hobnobs are safe in the tin.

I keep the photocopier on for company.
I sit in reception in slippers and a sunhat,
sipping Prosecco, as emails flood the server
and calls re-route to elsewhere.
I sweep spiders out of conference rooms
and settle down to snooze.

The last cleaner went in August,
with the man who watered the window-box.
The meter is read remotely now.
Each year I renew the insurance
and apply for subsidised travel.
Sometimes I re-order stationery.

Fire drill is on Thursdays.
I pull on my yellow marshal's jacket,
walk calmly to the empty car park,
and note my evacuation time.
I mark myself safe on Facebook.
I never use the lift.

Passing the Ball
Konstandinos Mahoney

Eight sharp, Sunday mornings,
I stand, spick and span by
tight tucked bed, hospital corners,
buffed leather.

Stiff-backed, clipped tache he comes
reeking of bay rum, inspects fold of sheet,
shine of shoe, checks under bed
for presence of dust.

One Sunday, no show.
At breakfast, stares at egg and bacon.
Asked what's wrong, says he's had a dream,
(shocked to learn he has such things as dreams)

they're hiding behind dunes,
waiting for a lull to swim to boats
moored offshore. They make a dash,
a shell explodes, his best mate's head

goes flying through the air,
"like a football," he says.
That night, a ball lands at my feet,
looks up wide-eyed and tries to speak.

The Hold Days
Geraldine Clarkson

All the lagging little children
marked with measles and pox
played in the red-brick courtyard
waiting for the ship's barping horn
to signal their return to the hold
where Captains in stained uniforms
gave them ointment and undiluted
rum, and told them winding stories
of the Cape, and sea-monsters, and home.
They were invited up on deck, protected
by windcheaters and the ship's cook, who
saved biscuits for their broth and stroked
their curving shoulders and tiny hunchbacks
bony as storks and marvelled at their
white hair and pus-lined eyes. A kiss
at times escaped him for the smallest
and sickliest of the group, for the tiniest
moment. *Forgive me,* he muttered
into a crusty scalp: *Bosun Billy's not
a bully.* And cloudy eyes would flicker
and hold his gaze with runtish hope.

Jeanne d'Arc on Flight TK1828
Antony Mair

A vision started it all – a shimmer at
the edge of a field, a voice that brushed her ear,
strange shadows dancing in a shaft of light
who took her in their arms. You're young, like her,

and when we check in I'm surprised you're alone.
You adjust your headscarf, walk off with your boarding card,
anonymous in your *abaya*, like a nun.
On the flight I watch you, wondering if you've heard

voices like those Jeanne spoke of, which press
against your skull. When we land at Istanbul
a young man, bearded, seems to check your face
against his phone, then waves, but doesn't smile.

As you leave with him, I think of the day when I
felt light flood through my ribs, and heard a voice
instruct me. Does everything seem clear to you
as it did to me? did they talk of sacrifice,

and secrets? Later I saw how small a spark
can trip the brain's tight circuits, darken the sun
and conceal demons with a conjuring trick.
When the flames lifted Jeanne's hair into a crown

I ask myself now if at last she understood
she'd been deluded by turns of the twisting mind;
if she wept for the victims she'd never prophesied,
caught in her dreams, ashes blown in the wind.

Women's Arts Alliance Exhibition 1975
Caroline Gilfillan

Look: a squished-up line
of kitchen utensils wonky as bunioned feet
with the instruction
Please play these with a wooden spoon

Listen. Listen hard. Clack-clack
of a knife chopping cabbage in a colander.
Sluggish swim of fork tines creaming mash.
Whir-whir shoosh of a racing whisk
seeding froth in evaporated milk to make it go further.

Let me praise women tied into aprons in sweltering kitchens –
mums, aunties, busty family friends –
who made cheese on toast
with a smear of fiery mustard,
who boiled up the lava of jam tarts.

Know that we struck and shook and rattled your utensils
till their metal clatter
ran down the stairs and through old-gent London streets
whose flat fronts were in need of a stitch and a polish.

Can you hear our blows, our hoo-hah,
as you lean towards two-bar electric fires,
knitting lumpy jumpers for girls who couldn't settle at home
like tabbies by the fire
but instead are prowling round London, caterwauling?

Out of the Blue
Lesley Saunders

– meaning how invention can be simply
the discovery of what was already there
awaiting us in the shadow: not a blank page

so much as an unborn child whose face
will swim into focus if we can hold our gaze
steady enough and for as long as it takes;

or how, when we wake to the grey,
we tread on a dream's fast-vanishing tail
to keep it from dulling to nothingness;

oh and how, on an evening like this,
all woodsmoke and stardust, the blue's
released from earth's iron to inscribe

light that will last, to catch the likeness
of a face that was loved; to print the past
on the present, forget-me-not, azure, exact.

*John Herschel, son of William and Mary Herschel, is credited with having invented
(or discovered) the cyanotype photographic process, now known as 'blueprint'.*

in the misperception of my life
Michèle Betty

after Adrienne Rich, "A clearing in the imagination"

I

mis
per
cep
tion
mist
aken
mis
prision
mi
scon
duct
mis
rep
resent
ation
mis
con
strue
mis
guide

II

in the misperception of my life
i mistake being alive
for wholeness, youth for ability
misperceiving
the gravity of the sea

for consistency, forgetting
the iceberg;
and as i struggle, i mis-
perceive dough for bread
neglect the benefits
of the warming oven;
in misperception
I run along footpaths,
not in the feline
undergrowth of the forest
floor, but out in the open
exposed to the elements
gifts upon misprision growing
misprision all about me
delusion rushing upon me
as I wade through its slush
ruthlessly rising to my necknape.

III

beguile; betray; cheat; confound;
deceive; delude; dupe; error;
fake; fallacy; fault; falsehood;
illude; outfox; trick; unfound.

Tied Up
Oliver Comins

This occurred part way through that tidal sweep
to containers: an entrance down a side-alley
jammed between terrace ends, then a glimpse
of harbour cranes on a quayside down the hill.
One of us had heard about it from a relative,
a wayward aunt or uncle who knew too much
and lived to tell the tale. Another of our group
had telephoned a friend, starting up a tenuous
chain of contacts through whom we assembled
a convincing narrative from multiple fragments.

We already knew how to obtain mission-critical
information from other peoples' ramblings —
how their stories of unrelated events or places
would expose half-spoken truths about which
we could not ask explicitly. Someone's bland
description of a taxi ride revealed the street,
then another teller's slice of history innocently
gave us the window, its view across the estuary.
We'd played the lottery for years and reconciled
ourselves to that sense of loss as future gain.

The island's value was derived from where it lay
relative to other places, not on what it was itself –
a destination of a kind, with wealth acquired
from movement through its dependable waters.
A fee fell due on tying up. No-one disembarked
without some sort of payment being processed.
Any act of landing goods was settled promptly
in cash or kind, the latter through a promissory
handled by an appointed expert whose knowledge
of value in most items would not be challenged.

Later generations struggled – could not agree
how to approach the changing pattern of trade.
A reduction in some numbers alarmed them,
even if overall volume was expected to grow
significantly. New skills would be required
and new facilities, but no commitment was made
to flatten and extend the headland down river.
Decay is never instant: railings only rusted slowly,
paintwork faded and small plants grew in walls
where people moved less often and less urgently.

In Crimson Boots
Jo Sanders

I stretch, step backwards
crunching pumice
and layers of ash.
I turn around.
The elegant red, stained
grim and grimy.
On the changing ground
toes are fragile
ankle bones coiling.
Boots have shrunk,
their tongues hiss
the eyes flick.
Cranes circle , shrill
in the absence of sound.
Cruelty ripples in the dark.

Homecoming
Mark Huband

Frost had chewed the magnolia petals, now rotting like jagged teeth.

It was winter when I had last seen them,
when the spike cold had still crawled among the tight-closed
mouths of the early tulips,
before light and dusk and dark were sealed
beyond the half-closed blinds of the white room.

Visitors no longer bring flowers for the sick.
Stems do not wilt.
Leaves do not wither.
Petals do not fade.

Twilight had mellowed the space within my walls.
A voice called to another.
A door slipped shut.
Numbers rose and fell as measures of progress.
Blood was taken. More blood, from the collapsing veins of a
bruised arm,
time measured in blood's tell-tale signs of recovery.

And when the numbers calmed and the blood cooled,
and the clock ticked to the breath and the heart
and the window light
no longer beat
to the stuttering rhythm of night and morning,
a sharp voice spoke of going home.

Of home.

Time had been the linoleum length of a disinfected corridor.
Time became the sun of late afternoon as it warmed my face.
The petals of the magnolia are falling.

Laughter roars from the gaping throats of the tulips.

Dancing the Harvest In
Brian Docherty

(after Keith Tyson, *Under A Harvest Moon He Works 24 Hours A Day . . .*)

I'm still not sure what happened in that field
or whether I dreamt it while lying in a ditch

on the way home from *The Stag*; my good wife
says she left me talking to some Morris dancers,

went home to watch a *Midsomer Murders* repeat,
found me seated at the kitchen table gone 4 am.

I was wet, cold, muddy, but otherwise unharmed,
apart from this green rune gracing my forehead.

Was that personage under the full moon a demon,
a Green Man gone feral, or a local prank aimed at

outlandish folks like me? Whoever or whatever,
he danced across the field, out and back, round

and round, his naked feet crunched the stubble,
curled up & pointed like mediaeval shoes, moving

to a music only he could hear, red mouth leering,
long pitchfork miming a sea sprite's trident, is he

the mermaids' cousin, and what was in his left hand?
Under that moon, it could have been a bat, a bottle,

or something mortal folk do not need to know about,
only be thankful it is not aimed at them in earnest.

As for his work, as long as the beer & bread are good,
my friends will welcome his avatar at Jack in the Green.

Empty Box (Death Of A Cat)
Arthur Fox

The vet came out and said "I'm sorry son"
Then, handing back the empty box, he said
"There's nothing I could do for him, the wound's
Too bad." I looked and thought that he had lied
'Cos you had been alive although you cried
Inside the box I'd carted all the way from home.
I'd found you in the garden lying down,
Your leg a mess of blood and exposed bone.
I used a kitchen cloth to wrap your leg
And placed you on a cushion in a box
I'd emptied my old tin toy soldiers out.
An afterthought put airholes in the lid.
So I was pretty sure you'd be O.K..
Silent, I looked at him in disbelief.
He looked at me askance and walked away.

I hugged the box, walked slowly through the park
And felt you move, imagined you alive,
Although I knew it was the cushion that had moved
From side to side. I did not know that I could name a cat
When you wandered in, a stray. Mum said
You were a tabby, but I misheard the word
And so I called you Tubby, although you were not fat.

I placed the box back by the fire where you
Had slept and for a while I looked at it.
What had killed you? Probably a fox.
More sorry for myself than for my cat
Defeated in my plan to save his life
A while I sat and then returned
My soldiers to their box.

Hairy Panic
Matt Barnard

When hairy panic rolled into Wagga Wagga
and filled up doorways and smothered cars
and overwhelmed the gardens, it felt like
the world had ended and not ended too.
It felt like the whole town was under water.

People didn't know what to do with themselves,
whether to fold up their lives and leave them
in the back of a drawer. To shed their loose skin
and run naked up the high street, into the banks,
up and down the whole food aisles in supermarkets.

Even the animals were lost, dogs gone wild
yellow big heads mooning about the place.
One man tried to shoot himself, but used
the wrong end of a banana. Someone announced
the second coming, but no one believed them.

As lazy-eyed Pete said, a case of too many
kangaroos loose in the top paddock, mate.

Among the Translators
David Underdown

We sat together in that airless hall
to spell out justifications for what we do,
how we mould the words of one language
into words of another that are easy on the ear
for readers who seek instruction or amusement
and each of us in a poor way striving merely to be of use,
and he allowing his head to fall while the minutes lengthened
and his face to sink into a mask, let no hint slip of his intentions,
but of an instant bolted up and spoke, his eyes sharp and full of the blaze
of how the people have been seized by such hate of what is foreign to them,
have turned in upon themselves against whoever they think should no longer
    be their concern
blaming them as if it is their fault, this new-found misery
and how it is the need, the task of all who work with words
not to let their meaning slip or disallow their angularity or carefulness
and especially if those words speak of suffering or anger at the plight of others
or of fellows, or of loved ones, or even of themselves,
it is needful to speak out what is true.
And as he spoke we all fell silent
and looking at each other knew.

On the journey home
Jack Houston

Round the roundabout. Again. Millie. Brake.
White Mazda pulls in front. Plastic-wrap
of yellow chrysanthemums slips
from the passenger seat into the foot-well.
Millie's little smile. Flowers.
Brighten up the flat, the flat shared with Alex, their flat.
That exit there, down what would have been the second exit.
How many times past it now?
A long shift. Millie's little laugh.
At work. Maybe that's it.
Think of Mum's, think of popping off at this next exit here,
there, down there and past the woods and the under-fives playground,
behind the school. Millie's school.
Blue saloon, Merc, swings in front, swings out again, knows where it's going.
Millie, fizzy little Millie.
Grip the wheel. Keep turning. Her grin and her 'Hello Ro'
every morning, giggling up, even through the drips
and the ventilator. Round and round, the exit signs pointing out
places not near here. Her parents didn't come in much.
At the end. Terrible. Some don't. Parents. Can't face it.
Want to leave it until it's too little too late
so they can really rip themselves apart with the guilt.
Maybe just can't face watching something so precious
fade like cut flowers. Swoosh the windows with cleaner,
wiper it off. A sculpture, some topiary, cut into the shape of a rabbit.
In the middle of the roundabout. Her sparkle remained though,
right to the finish. Playing with her stuffed bunny, Jessie,
the one her nan had given her. Should be used to this by now.
Turn on the radio, there's a song, course there is, turn it off.
Sàt in the hospice lunch hall, all of us, the nurses,
the other kids, the upstairs staff, eating lunch,
Millie making everyone laugh.

Millie playing with her bread roll, making it a mouse,
        pretending to scare us.
Millie. Millie. Millie.
There's a sign on the main exit,
the exit that leads back to the motorway.
For services. Where the flowers came from.
She closed her eyes, Millie, that last time, holding my hand.
We held hands. A fourth exit. Never gone that way.
Think you know a place. Reach for the indicator.

LIVE CANON